How Graphics Cards Really Work

The Hardware Driving Gaming, AI, and Real-Time Visualization

Emas Oyaks

Disclaimer

This book is intended for informational and educational purposes only. While every effort has been made to ensure the accuracy, reliability, and completeness of the content, the author and publisher make no representations or warranties regarding the applicability of the material in specific situations or for individual use cases.

Readers are encouraged to conduct their own research and consult with certified professionals before making technical, financial, or investment decisions based on the information presented in this publication. The author and publisher disclaim any liability for any direct, indirect, incidental, or consequential loss or damage incurred by any person relying on the information provided in this book.

Mention of specific brands, products, companies, or technologies is for reference purposes only and does not imply endorsement or affiliation.

All trademarks and registered trademarks are the property of their respective owners.

Copyright

Table OF Contents

Introduction

The hum of a computer used to be a simple sound—a machine flickering to life to run spreadsheets, compose letters, maybe play a few pixelated games. But today, that familiar hum has transformed into the roar of an engine, one capable of constructing entire worlds, painting lifelike portraits in real time, predicting the future through AI, and visualizing the unimaginable. At the heart of it all, almost like a pulse in the veins of modern technology, is the graphics card.

Once upon a time, graphics cards were humble components. Their only job was to throw a few colors onto a screen, to help a computer show text a little faster, or animate a simple sprite across a pixelated background. They weren't glamorous. They weren't powerful. They were sidekicks, background players, working behind the scenes. But as the ambitions of humanity grew—bigger games, richer storytelling, deeper simulations—something extraordinary happened. These once-simple circuits evolved into titans.

Today, graphics cards aren't just about "graphics" anymore. They are engines of computation, capable of crunching billions of operations in a single second. They simulate physical realities, model human thought, forecast natural disasters, and create cinematic experiences once reserved for Hollywood's biggest studios—all in the devices we carry into our homes. If technology has a soul, then in many ways, it's the GPU.

Think about the last time a video game left you breathless—the shimmer of water under a digital sun, the gust of wind through a hero's hair, the tiny imperfections on the blade of a sword. All of that exists not because someone painted each pixel by hand, but because a graphics card calculated, assembled, and delivered those realities to your eyes, faster than your brain could question whether it was real.

Or think about the breakthrough moments in medicine—surgeons using virtual reality to practice operations, AI models diagnosing cancer years earlier than humans could, weather systems predicting storms with pinpoint accuracy. Behind each of these triumphs is a GPU working tirelessly, unseen, but utterly indispensable.

Graphics cards have become the secret weapon of the modern world.

They are the reason games are immersive, why filmmakers can conjure dragons and alien planets with breathtaking realism, why scientists can simulate the birth of galaxies or map the human brain neuron by neuron. They power the artificial intelligences that will define the future. They turn dreams into reality, pixels into worlds, and raw data into discovery.

This book isn't just about explaining how graphics cards work. It's about peeling back the curtain on the most awe-inspiring piece of technology that most people never even think about. It's about understanding the magic—because once you know what's happening under the hood, you'll never look at your computer, your console, or even your smartphone the same way again.

We'll journey from the early days of simple 2D accelerators, when the idea of "real-time 3D" was the stuff of fantasy, to the current golden age of GPUs—where real-time ray tracing, AI-driven upscaling, and neural rendering are redefining what's possible in real time. We'll dive deep into the core components of a graphics card: the silicon heart, the memory brain, the cooling lungs that prevent it from melting under pressure. You'll see how thousands of tiny cores work in parallel to accomplish what once took entire supercomputers.

You'll discover how gaming pushed GPUs into greatness—and how artificial intelligence hijacked that greatness for even more profound ends.

We'll explore how rendering works from the inside out: how a mesh of points becomes a 3D object, how that object gets lit, textured, and finally turned into the breathtaking visuals you see on a monitor. You'll see how specialized cores, like ray-tracing units and tensor processors, elevate the GPU into realms of realism and computation that were science fiction a decade ago.

But we won't stop there. This book also opens the door to the future. You'll see how cloud gaming is rewriting the rules of ownership, how virtual and augmented reality are redefining immersion, and how GPUs are helping scientists and engineers tackle humanity's biggest problems—from climate change to cancer research.

And for those who crave not just understanding but mastery, we'll dive into the world of tuning and overclocking—where enthusiasts push their cards to the absolute limits, chasing every last drop of performance. You'll learn how graphics cards are designed, manufactured, tested, and tuned before they ever land in a gamer's rig or an AI researcher's server farm.

You don't need to be an engineer to appreciate this journey. You only need curiosity—and maybe, by the end of it, a touch of reverence for the tiny, brilliant miracle ticking inside your machine.

Because the truth is, graphics cards aren't just about better frame rates or shinier pixels. They are about possibility. About standing at the edge of what we can imagine—and then building it. They represent one of the purest intersections of art and science humanity has ever created.

And once you truly understand what's happening inside a graphics card, you'll realize: You've been living alongside silent, tireless architects of the future all along.

So buckle up.
The pixels await.
And reality? It's about to get even more extraordinary.

Chapter 1

The Evolution of Graphics Cards

The story of graphics cards is a thrilling reflection of humanity's relentless quest for visual perfection and faster, more powerful machines. From the earliest, flickering displays of simple pixels to today's stunningly realistic, immersive virtual worlds, the journey of graphics processing units (GPUs) captures the spirit of technological innovation like few others. When early computers began to emerge in the mid-20th century, their creators focused primarily on computation—solving mathematical problems, analyzing data, or running simple text-based programs. Visual representation, if it existed at all, was an afterthought.

Yet even in those primitive days, the seeds of a graphics revolution were quietly being planted. Engineers realized that humans are visual creatures, and if computers were to become more than just tools for scientists and mathematicians, they would have to speak in images. The primitive monochrome monitors gave way to colored screens, and bit by bit, technology learned to paint with pixels. Slowly, the dream of rendering complex visual worlds came closer to reality.

The transformation of computer graphics would not be a simple evolution; it would be a series of bold leaps forward. Each new breakthrough—from 2D acceleration to 3D rendering, from shaders to ray tracing, and now the explosion of artificial intelligence applications—built upon the foundations laid by earlier pioneers. In a sense, the evolution of the GPU mirrors the evolution of human creativity itself: always reaching for more detail, more realism, more emotion.

Today, graphics cards are no longer just about games or flashy visuals. They have become essential engines of innovation across industries as diverse as medicine, autonomous vehicles, scientific research, film production, and financial modeling. GPUs have transcended their original purpose, becoming the heart of the new computational era. But to truly appreciate their remarkable journey, one must go back to where it all began—with the humble beginnings of early computer graphics.

Early Computer Graphics and 2D Acceleration

In the beginning, computer graphics were rudimentary and utilitarian. The earliest displays were little more than oscilloscopes adapted to show simple lines and dots. Systems like the Whirlwind I, developed at MIT in the 1950s, could display basic graphical output, but the concept of rich, interactive visuals was still a distant dream. What mattered then was functionality, not aesthetic beauty.

The 1970s saw a notable shift. As computers like the Xerox Alto introduced graphical user interfaces (GUIs), the need for better visual output grew. Engineers developed simple framebuffers—sections of memory used specifically to store images. These innovations laid the groundwork for the concept of hardware dedicated to handling visual data.

However, these early systems placed heavy burdens on the central processing unit (CPU). All drawing tasks, from rendering text to plotting lines and shapes, were handled by the CPU itself, severely limiting the complexity and speed of graphics. This bottleneck became more pronounced as graphical demands increased with the rise of personal computing in the late 1970s and early 1980s.

Enter 2D acceleration. The concept was simple yet revolutionary: instead of burdening the CPU with every graphical task, a separate chip—dedicated solely to accelerating 2D operations—could take over some of the workload. The IBM 8514 graphics card, released in 1987, became one of the first mass-market accelerators capable of offloading basic functions like line drawing, bit blitting (moving large blocks of data across memory), and window management.

This change unleashed a wave of innovation. Companies like S3 Graphics, Matrox, and ATI Technologies (later acquired by AMD) emerged, offering products that could dramatically improve the speed and quality of 2D graphics. Suddenly, using a computer wasn't just about typing commands into a dark screen; it became a visually rich experience. Color depths increased from 16 colors to 256 and beyond, screen resolutions climbed, and graphical interfaces became more fluid and engaging.

The rise of 2D acceleration also set the stage for an even more ambitious leap: the move into the third dimension. By proving that graphical tasks could be separated from the CPU and handled by specialized hardware, developers laid the blueprint for the GPUs of the future. They just didn't realize yet how much more incredible that future would become.

The Rise of 3D Graphics and Real-Time Rendering

The transition from flat, two-dimensional imagery to fully immersive three-dimensional environments marks one of the most dramatic shifts in computer history. As early as the 1970s, researchers experimented with 3D graphics, producing crude wireframe models for military and scientific simulations. Yet for everyday users, 3D seemed like science fiction—a luxury confined to big-budget laboratories.

By the early 1990s, however, things began to change. Advances in silicon manufacturing, memory, and computational design made it feasible to imagine real-time 3D rendering on consumer hardware. The gaming industry, always hungry for new ways to captivate players, led the charge. Titles like Doom (1993) and Quake (1996) became cultural phenomena, proving that even basic 3D environments could create astonishingly immersive experiences.

At the heart of this revolution was the realization that 3D graphics demanded an entirely new type of hardware. Unlike 2D acceleration—which mostly involved copying and manipulating blocks of pixels—3D rendering required complex mathematical operations: matrix transformations, lighting calculations, texture mapping, and shading.

CPUs, even when helped by 2D accelerators, simply couldn't handle the load.

Thus, true graphics processing units (GPUs) were born. Companies like 3dfx Interactive, with its iconic Voodoo graphics cards, redefined gaming by introducing dedicated 3D acceleration hardware. Meanwhile, NVIDIA and ATI were developing their own technologies, steadily raising the bar for performance and visual fidelity.

What made these early GPUs revolutionary was their ability to perform real-time rendering. Rather than calculating and displaying frames one at a time (a slow, laborious process in earlier systems), GPUs could generate frames fast enough to respond instantly to user input. This unlocked entirely new kinds of experiences—fluid, responsive, and exhilarating.

Real-time 3D rendering would become the backbone not only of gaming but of countless other fields, from architecture to virtual reality. It changed how people interacted with technology, opening doors to previously unimaginable virtual worlds. And it was just the beginning.

Key Innovations: Shaders, Parallelism, Ray Tracing

As GPUs matured, so did their sophistication. No longer content with merely pushing more polygons to the screen, developers and engineers sought to create graphics that could mimic the subtleties of real life: the shimmer of water, the softness of fabric, the complex interplay of light and shadow.

Central to this next leap were shaders. Introduced in the late 1990s and early 2000s, shaders allowed developers to write small programs that dictated exactly how surfaces appeared. Instead of relying on pre-set behaviors, artists and programmers could craft materials that reacted dynamically to lighting, weather, or even user interactions. Games like Half-Life 2 and Crysis showcased stunningly realistic environments, thanks largely to sophisticated shader techniques.

Meanwhile, parallelism became the watchword of GPU design. Traditional CPUs processed tasks sequentially, handling one instruction at a time at extremely high speeds. GPUs, by contrast, were optimized to handle thousands—or even millions—of operations simultaneously. This made them extraordinarily powerful for the highly parallel nature of graphics rendering, where every pixel or vertex might need its own calculation.

The benefits of parallelism extended far beyond visuals. Researchers soon realized that GPUs could be adapted for general-purpose computation (a field known as GPGPU). Suddenly, GPUs were being used to simulate complex physical systems, analyze financial data, and even train neural networks.

Finally, there was the long-sought Holy Grail of graphics realism: ray tracing. Unlike traditional rasterization, which approximates the way light interacts with objects, ray tracing simulates the actual paths of photons as they bounce through a scene. The results are breathtakingly realistic, with accurate reflections, refractions, and shadows.

For decades, ray tracing was too computationally expensive for real-time applications. But breakthroughs by companies like NVIDIA, which introduced RTX technology in 2018, changed the game. Today, gamers and professionals alike can experience the magic of real-time ray-traced graphics—bringing virtual worlds closer than ever to photorealism.

GPUs in the Era of AI and Visualization

In the 2020s, graphics cards have transcended their original mission altogether. While they still power incredible gaming experiences and dazzling digital art, they have become indispensable engines for artificial intelligence and scientific visualization.

At the core of this transformation is the GPU's unparalleled ability to handle massive amounts of data in parallel. Training a deep learning model requires processing millions of parameters across huge datasets—a task perfectly suited to the architecture of modern GPUs. Without GPUs, the AI revolution would have stalled before it ever began.

Today, GPUs are the beating heart behind systems that drive self-driving cars, power voice recognition assistants, detect diseases from medical images, and even generate realistic human faces through generative adversarial networks (GANs). Technologies like NVIDIA's CUDA and AMD's ROCm have opened GPUs to a wider audience of researchers and developers, sparking innovation across countless fields.

Visualization has also entered a new golden age, fueled by the power of GPUs. Scientists now create breathtakingly detailed simulations of galaxies, weather patterns, and molecular structures. Engineers design complex machinery with unprecedented accuracy through virtual prototyping. Architects and artists collaborate in virtual environments that look and feel almost indistinguishable from the real world.

The evolution of the graphics card—from a humble 2D accelerator to the centerpiece of global innovation—illustrates a profound truth: technology, when fueled by imagination and ambition, can change not just what we see, but how we think, create, and dream.

Chapter 2

Anatomy of a Graphics Card

The intricate world of graphics cards stands at the heart of modern computing, a technological marvel that has steadily evolved into a critical component of nearly every personal computer and workstation. For gamers seeking breathtaking visuals, designers demanding flawless renderings, or researchers tackling immense datasets, the graphics card has become indispensable. It's not merely a piece of silicon tucked inside a machine; it's the lifeblood of modern digital experiences, fueling everything from photorealistic gaming landscapes to breakthroughs in artificial intelligence.

When someone gazes at a graphics card, they often see only a sleek, sometimes colorful, device adorned with fans, RGB lighting, and branding. Beneath that external shell lies an intricate world of engineering brilliance. The graphics card orchestrates millions of calculations every second, interprets complex instructions, and translates mathematical data into the images that captivate our eyes. This orchestration doesn't happen by chance—it is the result of a carefully balanced blend of processing power, memory bandwidth, thermal control, power management, and specialized acceleration units.

Understanding the anatomy of a graphics card isn't just a technical exercise; it's a way of appreciating the synergy between multiple systems working in harmony. Each component, from the mighty GPU at its core to the specialized tensor cores at the periphery, plays a crucial role in delivering the jaw-dropping performance users have come to expect. Every wire, every solder point, every fan blade has a purpose—fine-tuned over decades of innovation.

The evolution of the graphics card mirrors the ever-growing hunger for more immersive digital experiences. Early GPUs barely managed to render basic 2D graphics; today's versions handle billions of polygons per second, simulate realistic lighting through ray tracing, and even participate in training complex neural networks. As technology continues to advance, the graphics card becomes not just a tool but a symbol of progress, unlocking new dimensions in entertainment, productivity, and scientific discovery.

In this chapter, we'll journey deep inside the graphics card, breaking it down part by part. We'll explore how each element fits together to create a unified whole capable of transforming zeros and ones into living, breathing digital worlds. Whether you're a curious enthusiast, a gamer upgrading your rig, or someone who simply wants to understand the technology powering the future, this exploration offers a front-row seat to the ingenuity behind every frame your eyes see on a screen.

The Heart: The Graphics Processing Unit (GPU)

At the very core of every graphics card lies the Graphics Processing Unit—the engine where dreams are rendered into visible reality. A piece of silicon no larger than a postage stamp, yet packed with billions of microscopic transistors, the GPU handles an unimaginable volume of operations every second. It is the beating heart that powers the awe-inspiring visuals we see in modern games, immersive virtual environments, and sophisticated visual effects.

Unlike a traditional CPU, which handles tasks sequentially with extreme focus, the GPU thrives on parallelism. It's designed to perform thousands—sometimes millions—of small calculations at the same time. Picture a CPU as a brilliant mathematician working through problems methodically, while the GPU operates like an entire stadium full of skilled problem-solvers, each tackling a small piece simultaneously. This ability makes GPUs extraordinarily efficient for rendering graphics, where every pixel, vertex, and texture requires rapid processing.

Deep inside, a GPU is organized into clusters of cores—simple yet highly specialized processors that work together to manage rendering pipelines. These pipelines involve multiple stages: geometry processing to define shapes, rasterization to transform 3D models into 2D representations, shading to simulate light interaction, and post-processing effects to polish the final image. Each of these stages demands intense mathematical work, and the GPU handles it with remarkable finesse.

Over the years, GPU architecture has evolved to incorporate highly modular and scalable designs. Modern GPUs from companies like NVIDIA and AMD use designs based on Compute Units (CUs) or Streaming Multiprocessors (SMs), where hundreds of tiny cores operate in harmony. These designs allow for scaling from compact mobile GPUs to massive workstation cards without fundamentally altering the architectural principles.

Another remarkable feature of the GPU is its programmable shaders. In the early days, graphics chips had fixed-function pipelines—rigid designs where certain stages could not be altered. Today's GPUs allow programmers to write customized shaders—small programs that determine how every pixel and vertex behaves. This flexibility opened the doors to cinematic realism, with developers crafting intricate effects like dynamic lighting, shadow casting, water reflections, and physically based rendering.

GPUs are not just graphics processors anymore. Their architecture, optimized for parallel tasks, has made them essential in fields far beyond gaming. Machine learning, cryptography, physics simulations, medical imaging—many industries now leverage the power of GPUs to solve complex problems faster than traditional CPUs could dream of.

Clock speeds, measured in MHz or GHz, define how fast the GPU's internal cores operate. Higher clock speeds generally translate to better performance, but it's not the only factor. Architectural efficiency, memory bandwidth, core counts, and thermal management all influence how well a GPU performs in the real world.

In addition to traditional rasterized rendering, modern GPUs support advanced techniques such as ray tracing—an approach that simulates the behavior of light with almost photographic realism. This capability, once considered the holy grail of computer graphics, has now become mainstream, thanks to innovations within the GPU's fundamental architecture.

Power consumption and heat generation are natural byproducts of such intense computational effort. As a result, GPUs come equipped with sophisticated thermal management systems and often require significant power delivery solutions to sustain peak performance. These topics, along with others like VRAM (Video RAM), specialized cores, and cooling technologies, create the intricate dance that allows the GPU to function seamlessly.

The Graphics Processing Unit remains one of the most fascinating pieces of technology today, combining art and science into a masterpiece of modern engineering. It's a testament to human ingenuity—a living reminder that at the crossroads of mathematics, physics, and creativity lies a spark capable of bringing entire worlds to life on our screens.

Memory Matters: VRAM and Bandwidth

While the Graphics Processing Unit (GPU) serves as the dynamic brain of a graphics card, it relies heavily on another essential partner to perform its miracles—memory. Known as VRAM (Video Random Access Memory), this dedicated memory works hand in glove with the GPU, ensuring that an ocean of textures, models, lighting maps, and frame buffers can be accessed at lightning speed. Without high-speed VRAM, even the most powerful GPU would stagger under the weight of modern graphics workloads, bottlenecked by the inability to move data swiftly enough.

Think of VRAM as the artist's palette in a grand studio. It's where all the paints—the textures, color data, geometry information, and lighting parameters—are laid out and readily available for the artist (the GPU) to pick and apply without delay. The bigger and faster the palette, the more complex and rich the masterpiece can become.

At the heart of VRAM's importance is its role as a frame buffer. Every image you see on your screen must first be composed in memory before it can be displayed. As games and applications push toward ever-higher resolutions—1440p, 4K, and beyond—the amount of memory needed to store these ultra-detailed frames grows exponentially. Running out of VRAM during heavy tasks forces the system to fall back on much slower system memory (RAM), causing stuttering, frame drops, and frustrating performance issues.

Modern graphics cards use specialized types of memory like GDDR6, GDDR6X, or HBM2 (High Bandwidth Memory) to meet these ever-increasing demands. Each generation brings faster speeds, lower latencies, and higher bandwidth. GDDR6X, for instance, utilizes advanced signalling

dramatically boosting the rate at which data can move between the GPU and its memory. This acceleration is critical because today's cutting-edge visuals—whether it's the hyper-realistic lighting in AAA games or the dense datasets in deep learning models—demand breathtaking memory performance to function smoothly.

Bandwidth, often overlooked by casual buyers, is just as important as the amount of VRAM itself. Bandwidth refers to the volume of information that can be read from or written to memory per second, and it is usually measured in gigabytes per second (GB/s). A card with high VRAM capacity but poor bandwidth is like a massive reservoir with a narrow pipeline: the resource is there, but getting it where it's needed becomes a bottleneck.

Take for example a memory bus width of 256 bits versus 384 bits. All else being equal, the wider bus allows more data to flow at once, similar to a multilane highway versus a single-lane road. When combined with high memory clock speeds, the result is breathtakingly fast data transfer rates, empowering the GPU to maintain fluid frame rates even under the most grueling workloads.

In real-world terms, a high-bandwidth graphics card allows you to play a fast-paced shooter at 4K resolution with ray tracing enabled without worrying about texture pop-ins or performance hitches. It ensures that massive open-world games feel seamless rather than disjointed. And for professionals, it guarantees that heavy 3D models or multi-layered video projects can be manipulated in real time, without the frustration of lag or delayed feedback.

Another key advancement that modern GPUs leverage is memory compression. Instead of blindly storing every bit of visual data at full size, intelligent compression algorithms reduce the memory footprint of textures and buffers without noticeable loss in quality. This clever trick effectively multiplies the available bandwidth and VRAM size, making operations faster and more efficient. It's an unseen but powerful ally working silently behind every detailed scene you experience.

As you climb the ladder of GPU classes—from entry-level models to top-tier enthusiast cards—you'll notice a steady increase not just in VRAM quantity but also in memory technology sophistication. Budget cards might offer 6GB to 8GB of GDDR6 memory running over a 128-bit bus, suitable for 1080p gaming. Mid-range cards typically boast 8GB to 12GB with faster clock speeds and wider buses, ideal for 1440p gaming and light professional tasks. Meanwhile, flagship models flaunt 16GB,

20GB, or even 24GB of the fastest GDDR6X or HBM2e memory across massive buses, preparing them for the rigors of 4K gaming, ray tracing, and advanced AI training.

Understanding VRAM requirements by workload can save you from costly mistakes. For example:

Casual 1080p gamers can thrive with 6GB–8GB of VRAM.

Competitive 1440p gamers will find 10GB–12GB ideal for high settings.

4K enthusiasts and content creators should prioritize 16GB or more.

Professional 3D rendering, simulation, or AI tasks often require 24GB+ for optimal results.

It's tempting to simply "buy the biggest number" when comparing VRAM capacities, but savvy buyers look deeper. They balance capacity with memory speed, bandwidth, bus width, and compression technologies to find a card that matches both their current needs and future ambitions. A well-chosen card ensures you can enjoy high-fidelity visuals and demanding applications today without facing painful upgrades just around the corner.

In the ever-evolving tech landscape, VRAM and bandwidth are the quiet forces determining whether your experience is immersive and fluid or stuttery and compromised. As 8K displays, real-time ray tracing, VR experiences, and AI-augmented graphics become mainstream, investing wisely in this area becomes not just smart—it becomes essential.

Because in the end, your graphics card's memory isn't just storing data—it's curating an experience. Every vivid sunset in a game, every intricate shadow in a 3D model, every ultra-crisp frame of a cinematic masterpiece relies on it working flawlessly. Understanding and appreciating VRAM and bandwidth elevates you from a passive user to an empowered architect of your digital experience.

Keeping It Cool: Cooling Systems and Heat Management

The heart of any high-performance system—especially when it comes to gaming, design, or AI tasks—requires not only power but also precision in managing heat. As graphics cards push the limits of performance, generating enormous amounts of processing power, the necessity for efficient cooling systems has become paramount. Without them, a powerful GPU would quickly overheat, leading to thermal throttling, reduced performance, or, in the worst case, permanent damage to the delicate components inside. Cooling is not just an accessory; it's the lifeline that ensures sustained, reliable performance.

When you observe the aesthetics of modern graphics cards, you'll often notice the intricate and imposing cooling systems—large fans, multiple heat pipes, and expansive heatsinks. But cooling solutions in GPUs go beyond their visual appeal. They are meticulously engineered to balance airflow, heat dissipation, and acoustics. Let's break down the elements that make these cooling systems so effective.

Fans and Heatsinks: The Basics of Cooling

The most visible part of a GPU's cooling system is its fans. These serve as the first line of defense against the heat generated by the processing power of the GPU. Whether they're traditional axial fans or more advanced blower fans, these cooling solutions help move air across the heatsink. The heatsink is a collection of metal fins designed to absorb and disperse heat efficiently. Heatpipes running through the heatsink carry the thermal energy from the GPU's core to the fins, allowing the heat to dissipate faster.

In high-performance graphics cards, the number of fans and the quality of the heatsink can significantly impact performance. More fans typically mean more airflow, but that also translates to more noise. In contrast, a high-quality heatsink can increase thermal efficiency while maintaining a quiet system. Some premium graphics cards feature dual or triple-fan setups designed to improve airflow and reduce the need for high RPMs, ensuring quieter operation without sacrificing cooling capacity.

Advanced Cooling: Vapor Chambers and Liquid Cooling

While traditional fans and heatsinks work for most users, extreme gamers and professionals often require more advanced solutions. Vapor chambers and liquid cooling systems are at the forefront of these innovations.

A vapor chamber operates on a principle similar to heatpipes but on a more expansive scale. This technology distributes heat more evenly over a larger surface area, increasing the efficiency of heat dissipation. Instead of relying on just one or two heatpipes, a vapor chamber uses a thin, sealed metal chamber that vaporizes the liquid inside, transferring heat away from the GPU before the vapor condenses back into a liquid. This cycle is incredibly efficient, ensuring that the GPU remains cool even under intense workloads.

For those who want the pinnacle of cooling performance, liquid cooling solutions—often found in custom or hybrid setups—offer unparalleled thermal management. These systems circulate liquid coolant through a closed-loop system, absorbing heat directly from the GPU and carrying it away to a radiator where it is cooled by fans. Liquid cooling is particularly valuable for users who push their GPUs to the extreme, such as when overclocking for high-end gaming or rendering.

Thermal Throttling: The Silent Performance Killer

If cooling systems fail to maintain optimal temperatures, the GPU resorts to thermal throttling. This is a built-in protective mechanism that reduces the GPU's clock speeds when it reaches unsafe temperatures. While throttling protects the hardware from overheating, it also causes a significant drop in performance, often resulting in choppy frame rates or stuttering during gameplay or rendering tasks.

Modern GPUs come with a built-in thermal sensor that constantly monitors the temperature and adjusts fan speeds or power consumption accordingly. However, even the most advanced cooling solutions can only manage temperatures within a specific range. If users push their GPUs beyond the thermal limits, throttling is inevitable. This is where choosing the right cooling solution becomes critical. High-performance GPUs are designed with more robust cooling in mind, but they rely on the user to ensure their PC case has enough airflow to support these systems.

Silent Operation vs. Performance: A Trade-Off

One of the most important considerations when selecting a GPU, especially for those building their systems, is the balance between cooling efficiency and noise levels. A quieter system is often preferred for a more comfortable working environment, but achieving silence can come at the cost of peak performance. GPUs with aggressive cooling solutions (e.g., multiple fans or liquid cooling) tend to produce more noise, especially when under load.

However, certain high-end models now feature semi-passive cooling, where fans remain off at low to moderate loads and only spin up under intense usage. This means your GPU operates silently during regular tasks like web browsing or light gaming, only ramping up when it's required for demanding workloads like 3D rendering or VR gaming.

Choosing the right balance between noise and cooling performance depends on the user's priorities. If you're a gamer looking for maximum performance at any cost, a louder cooling solution may be the way to go. But if you're someone who values a quieter system for work or casual entertainment, opting for a quieter, less aggressive cooling solution with good performance at moderate load might be the best choice.

Considerations for System Builders

When building or upgrading a system, cooling solutions need to be selected carefully. Case airflow is one of the most important aspects of overall cooling efficiency. A case with poor airflow will struggle to keep the GPU cool, regardless of the cooling solution inside the card itself. Ideally, you want a case with positive airflow, meaning intake fans at the front of the case and exhaust fans at the rear to help guide airflow through the system.

Additionally, if you're overclocking or pushing the GPU to its limits, additional case fans or even a dedicated cooling system (such as liquid cooling for the GPU) can make a big difference in maintaining stable temperatures.

For those looking for the ultimate cooling solution, some enthusiasts even opt for external GPU enclosures with liquid cooling. These enclosures remove heat away from the system entirely, further improving temperature management and extending the lifespan of the hardware.

Cooling Systems for Professional Users

Professional users, including those working in fields like 3D rendering, VR development, or AI research, often place higher demands on their GPUs than typical gamers. These users require stable, consistent performance over extended periods. The increased workloads from professional applications can drive GPUs to their thermal limits quickly. As such, ensuring the GPU stays cool during long render times, simulations, or training models is critical to both performance and longevity.

Professional-grade cooling solutions often feature larger heatsinks, more advanced vapor chamber designs, and the option to incorporate custom liquid cooling solutions. Additionally, many workstation-grade Gpus come equipped with active cooling for the memory and VRMs (Voltage Regulator Modules), which play crucial roles in maintaining stable power delivery to the GPU.

As technology advances, so do the cooling solutions, allowing for even higher performance with greater efficiency. With every new generation of Gpus, manufacturers continue to push the envelope on cooling design, helping users stay ahead of the curve. The modern GPU is as much a marvel of thermal engineering as it is a symbol of computational power.

Power Delivery and PCB Design

Every great technology needs a steady, reliable source of power to operate efficiently, and graphics cards are no exception. In fact, the power delivery system in a GPU is one of the most critical aspects of its performance and stability. Without a robust power system, even the most well-designed GPU would be unable to function at its full potential. This intricate dance between power delivery and the PCB (Printed Circuit Board) design is the backbone of a GPU's ability to deliver high-end performance in demanding tasks, from gaming to artificial intelligence research.

The power delivery system is responsible for providing the GPU with the appropriate voltage and current it requires to run, while the PCB acts as the nerve center, connecting all the components and ensuring that the power is distributed correctly. Together, they ensure the GPU operates at its best, regardless of the workload. Let's explore how these systems work together to support the raw power of modern GPUs.

The Role of Power Delivery in GPUs

The GPU's power delivery system is designed to ensure that the Graphics Processing Unit itself, along with all its auxiliary components such as the VRAM (Video Random Access Memory), receive a steady stream of power, regardless of fluctuations in system demand. Unlike simpler components like CPUs, which typically consume a more predictable amount of power,

GPUs are designed to handle wildly varying workloads. From simple tasks like rendering static images to complex operations such as real-time ray tracing or AI model training, the power system must adjust accordingly.

The voltage regulator module (VRM) is at the heart of this system. VRMs regulate and convert the voltage coming from your power supply to the specific levels needed by the GPU. As the GPU runs intensive tasks, it can draw a lot of power, so it's crucial that the VRM can supply this power reliably without overloading or causing instability. High-quality VRMs are essential for overclockers or users pushing their systems to the limit, as a stable power supply ensures the GPU's performance won't drop under pressure.

Phase design is also a critical element. The phase design refers to how many individual power delivery phases are included in the VRM design. Each phase is responsible for supplying a portion of the power to the GPU. Graphics cards with higher phase counts typically deliver more stable power, which is crucial for consistent performance, particularly under load. This becomes particularly relevant for enthusiasts who want to overclock their GPUs, as multiple phases help distribute the power demands and prevent overheating.

PCB Design: The Nervous System of a GPU

While power delivery ensures that a GPU receives the right amount of energy, the PCB (Printed Circuit Board) is the physical foundation that connects all the components, distributing both power and data to the GPU's cores, VRAM, and other essential components. The PCB is essentially the backbone of the graphics card, housing the various components in a carefully designed layout that maximizes both efficiency and performance.

The design and layout of the PCB are crucial for ensuring that the GPU runs at optimal speeds. A well-designed PCB helps to prevent signal interference, thermal hotspots, and other issues that could compromise performance. For instance, a poorly routed PCB can cause signal degradation as data travels from the GPU to VRAM, leading to lower performance. Advanced PCBs are meticulously engineered to reduce these losses, ensuring that data transfer between components is both fast and efficient. A well-optimized layout is key for the GPU's overall stability and speed, enabling it to handle the complex tasks required of modern graphics processing.

The PCB design also plays a vital role in managing heat. With modern GPUs pushing the limits of performance, thermal management is crucial. **Thermal pads**, **copper layers**, and **heat sinks** are often strategically placed across the PCB to facilitate efficient heat dissipation. The layout must account for hot spots, ensuring that the GPU's temperature remains stable and within safe operating limits to prevent throttling and damage to components.

Advanced PCB designs take into account not only the layout but also the **material** used for the board itself. For example, high-performance PCBs may incorporate **high-density interconnects** (HDI) and specialized materials like **ceramic** or **aluminum** substrates to improve heat dissipation and reduce signal loss. These materials help ensure that the GPU can maintain its high-speed operations while remaining cool, even under the most demanding workloads.

Power Connectors: Feeding the Beast

Another key component of the power delivery system is the **power connectors**. While the PCIe slot on the motherboard provides some power to the graphics card, high-end GPUs require more juice to run effectively. This is where external **6-pin, 8-pin, or even 12-pin PCIe connectors** come into play. These connectors allow the GPU to draw additional power directly from the power supply, ensuring it has the necessary resources to handle demanding applications such as 4K gaming, real-time ray tracing, and deep learning.

These connectors are vital for GPUs with high power demands. A **single 6-pin PCIe connector** can supply up to 75 watts, but when a GPU requires more power, additional connectors are added. GPUs with dual 8-pin connectors, for instance, can draw up to **300 watts**, which is necessary for overclocking or running the GPU at full capacity during intense computational tasks. The connectors provide flexibility, enabling users to scale the power delivery based on their performance needs.

Power connectors also help improve the **stability** and **reliability** of the GPU under load. A high-quality power delivery system, with robust and securely attached connectors, ensures that the GPU can draw consistent power without fluctuations that could lead to crashes, instability, or reduced performance.

Overclocking and Its Impact on Power Delivery

For those who seek to push their systems beyond the factory settings, **overclocking** is a popular option. Overclocking involves increasing the clock speeds of the GPU to improve its performance, but this comes at a cost. The GPU will demand more power, which puts additional strain on the power delivery system.

A GPU designed with a **high-quality VRM** and multiple **power phases** is better equipped to handle the increased power demands of overclocking. A stable power delivery system can supply the necessary power while preventing overheating, which is a common issue when overclocking. Some enthusiasts also rely on custom **liquid cooling solutions** or **advanced air cooling systems** to manage the added thermal load created by overclocking.

In addition to improving the power delivery, the **PCB layout** also plays a role in overclocking performance. A well-designed

PCB will have properly routed **power traces** and **heat dissipation channels**, helping the card maintain its stability even under extreme conditions. This is one of the reasons why high-end GPUs from manufacturers like ASUS, MSI, and EVGA often come with custom cooling solutions and enhanced PCBs tailored for overclocking.

Printed Circuit Board Layouts for Different GPU Tiers

The complexity of a GPU's PCB design varies depending on its target market. **Entry-level GPUs** generally have simpler PCBs, fewer power phases, and less complex routing, as they don't need to handle the high power demands of intensive tasks like gaming at 4K or running AI workloads. These cards are designed to offer a balance of performance and affordability, catering to users who don't need extreme graphics performance.

In contrast, **premium GPUs** intended for enthusiasts or professional users have much more intricate PCB designs. These cards feature additional power phases, specialized components for better heat dissipation, and more advanced routing techniques to ensure that the card can handle high-power workloads. The extra investment in a high-end GPU typically translates to **better overclocking potential, more consistent performance**, and improved **thermal efficiency**.

For example, **NVIDIA's Founders Edition cards** are often designed with a particular focus on both **aesthetic appeal** and **functional performance**, with custom PCBs that prioritize cooling and power delivery. These cards often feature **dual-fan cooling** systems or **blower-style cooling** that circulates air efficiently to manage heat. On the other hand, third-party designs from brands like MSI, ASUS, and Gigabyte tend to offer **more aggressive cooling solutions** and **higher-end PCB layouts** that push the limits of performance.

Ensuring Long-Term Reliability

Reliability is a crucial factor in the design of both power delivery systems and PCBs, as these components are under constant strain from continuous operation and fluctuating temperatures. Over time, power delivery components like **capacitors** and **inductors** can degrade, which could impact the GPU's overall performance. To combat this,

premium capacitors made of materials such as **solid aluminum** or **polymers** are used to extend the life of the card. These capacitors are built to handle higher temperatures and longer usage cycles, ensuring that the GPU remains stable and functional over time.

Additionally, **quality control** is essential in maintaining the integrity of these components. Manufacturers typically perform rigorous testing on power delivery systems and PCBs to ensure that they can withstand high levels of stress without failing. Testing for **thermal stress**, **electrical stability**, and **signal integrity** is a common practice, ensuring that users get a GPU that will function reliably even after years of heavy use.

Proper system maintenance, such as ensuring **adequate cooling** and **case ventilation**, can also extend the life of the power delivery system and PCB. By keeping the GPU at optimal temperatures, users can reduce the likelihood of **thermal damage** or **component wear** that could impact performance.

Specialized Units: Tensor Cores, RT Cores, and More

The evolution of modern graphics cards has ushered in a new era of specialized processing units designed to tackle specific types of workloads with unparalleled efficiency. Among these are Tensor Cores and RT Cores, which have significantly enhanced the capabilities of GPUs, pushing the boundaries of what's possible in real-time ray tracing, artificial intelligence, and machine learning. These specialized cores represent a shift from the traditional GPU design, which was once primarily focused on rendering graphics. Now, with these innovations, GPUs have become powerful multi-purpose processors capable of handling complex tasks far beyond gaming.

Tensor Cores: Revolutionizing AI and Deep Learning

Tensor Cores, first introduced by NVIDIA in their Volta architecture and later refined in the

Ampere and Ada Lovelace architectures, are designed specifically to accelerate tensor operations. Tensors, the multidimensional arrays at the heart of machine learning and artificial intelligence (AI) computations, require immense computational power to process. Tensor Cores take these operations and accelerate them by performing matrix multiplications at a much higher throughput than traditional CUDA cores.

In the context of AI, Tensor Cores are the unsung heroes behind deep learning tasks, such as training neural networks, object recognition, natural language processing, and more. The ability to perform thousands of calculations in parallel at lightning speeds makes Tensor Cores ideal for AI training and inference, particularly in real-time applications. For industries like autonomous vehicles, medical imaging, and financial modeling, the performance gains provided by Tensor Cores can be transformative, enabling faster model training and more accurate predictions.

The significance of Tensor Cores extends far beyond raw performance. These cores support mixed-precision computing, allowing them to operate with FP16 (half precision) and INT8 data formats. This capability enables more efficient AI processing by balancing performance and precision, enabling systems to handle even the most complex machine learning models while consuming less power.

As AI continues to play a pivotal role in various fields, Tensor Cores are positioning GPUs as essential tools not just for entertainment and design, but for scientific research, healthcare advancements, and data-driven innovations.

RT Cores: Pioneering Real-Time Ray Tracing

Real-Time Ray Tracing (RT) is one of the most exciting advancements in graphics rendering, providing incredibly realistic lighting, shadows, reflections, and global illumination effects. Unlike traditional rasterization methods, which approximate lighting based on pre-calculated data, ray tracing simulates the way light interacts with objects in a scene. This process, while capable of creating stunning visual effects, is computationally expensive—until the introduction of RT Cores.

NVIDIA's Turing architecture was the first to include dedicated RT Cores, designed specifically to accelerate ray tracing calculations. These cores are tasked with tracing the path of light rays as they bounce off surfaces and interact with materials, calculating reflections, refractions, and shadows in real-time. In modern games and simulations, RT Cores enable realistic lighting that dynamically adjusts to in-game actions, creating a far more immersive visual experience.

Ray tracing was once the domain of pre-rendered film studios due to the immense computational power required. However, with RT Cores integrated into GPUs, real-time ray tracing has become a staple in modern video games, bringing cinematic-quality visuals to interactive environments. The introduction of DLSS (Deep Learning Super Sampling) technology, which leverages Tensor Cores, further enhances the performance of ray tracing by upscaling lower-resolution images with AI-enhanced sharpness and detail.

For developers, RT Cores provide a powerful tool for crafting games with lifelike environments and lighting effects that respond to player actions. From reflections on water to realistic shadows in dynamic scenes, RT Cores are enabling a new level of graphical fidelity in real-time applications.

The Synergy Between Tensor Cores and RT Cores

While Tensor Cores and RT Cores serve distinct purposes, their combination unlocks new possibilities, particularly in next-generation gaming and professional applications. By offloading AI tasks to Tensor Cores and ray tracing calculations to RT Cores, GPUs can efficiently handle both demanding tasks simultaneously, without compromising on performance.

In gaming, this synergy allows for real-time ray-traced graphics alongside AI-enhanced features like intelligent NPC behavior and dynamic environmental effects. The use of AI in gaming has expanded beyond just graphics; it now encompasses elements like procedurally generated content, smarter AI enemies, and even AI-driven animation and facial expression systems. All of these are powered by the same Tensor Cores that fuel machine learning.

In professional applications such as architecture, product design, and film production, the combination of these specialized cores allows creators to work faster and with more accuracy. Real-time ray tracing and AI-powered tools streamline workflows by enabling faster previews, more precise simulations, and more intuitive design processes.

Specialized Cores for Future Technologies

The power of specialized cores in GPUs is not just limited to Tensor and RT Cores. As GPU technology continues to evolve, we are seeing new forms of specialized cores that target emerging fields and workloads. For example, NVIDIA's Ampere architecture introduced CUDA cores with enhanced AI capabilities, making GPUs even more versatile for scientific research, simulation modeling, and cloud computing.

The integration of AI-driven video encoding/decoding, hardware acceleration for blockchain mining, and even real-time 3D rendering for VR/AR applications showcases the growing flexibility of modern GPUs. The next generation of specialized cores will likely address even more niche demands, ranging from quantum computing to advanced robotics, as industries continue to embrace GPU acceleration for increasingly complex tasks.

Chapter 3

How Graphics Cards Render Worlds

When it comes to rendering the stunning worlds seen in modern games and simulations, graphics cards follow a highly specialized and efficient process known as the 3D graphics pipeline. This series of stages transforms raw 3D data—such as vertices, textures, and lighting information—into the vibrant, interactive images displayed on screens. Each step adds detail, realism, and precision, ensuring that the final output is not just visually impressive but also smooth and responsive.

The journey begins with vertex processing. Graphics cards first process the raw 3D data, taking individual points in 3D space called vertices and converting them into a format ready for screen rendering. This involves intricate mathematical operations that transform the vertices from their local object coordinates into world space, then into camera space, and finally into screen space. These transformations ensure that every object is correctly positioned and proportioned relative to the player's view, laying the groundwork for accurate rendering.

After vertex processing comes rasterization, where the GPU converts the processed vertices into fragments—the building blocks of pixels. Rasterization effectively fills in the shapes formed by vertices, preparing them for further refinement. It determines which pixels on the screen are covered by the shapes and interpolates properties such as texture coordinates, colors, and depth values across the surface. This critical stage marks the transformation from abstract 3D geometry to tangible 2D images, setting the stage for rich visual output.

With rasterization complete, shading takes over to define how surfaces interact with light. Shaders, small programs running on the GPU, calculate the final color and appearance of each fragment based on materials, lighting conditions, and view direction. Modern shading techniques, such as physically-based rendering (PBR), mimic the way light behaves in the real world, accounting for factors like metallic properties, roughness, and subsurface scattering. These advances result in surfaces that look convincingly real, whether it's the gleam of polished metal, the translucency of skin, or the shimmer of water.

While traditional rasterization and shading have powered graphics for decades, a new frontier emerged with real-time ray tracing. Unlike rasterization, which approximates lighting effects, ray tracing simulates the actual behavior of light. Rays are projected into a scene, bouncing off surfaces, refracting through transparent objects, and casting realistic shadows. This technique delivers stunning reflections, accurate global illumination, and natural-looking shadows, enhancing immersion to unprecedented levels. Hardware innovations, like dedicated RT Cores found in modern GPUs, have made it possible to achieve real-time ray tracing, a feat once thought impractical outside of film production.

Taking ray tracing even further is path tracing, a method that traces not just the direct paths of light rays but also their complex, multiple bounces throughout a scene. Path tracing captures intricate lighting phenomena such as caustics, soft shadows, and subtle color bleeding between surfaces. Although still extremely demanding, advancements in GPU technology are slowly bridging the gap, bringing elements of this gold-standard rendering technique into real-time applications, delivering visuals once limited to cinematic render farms.

Once all the rendering calculations are completed, the final stage involves outputting the finished frames to the display. This process is handled through frame buffers, which temporarily store the fully rendered images before sending them to the monitor. Frame buffers ensure that each complete frame is ready and correctly synchronized, preventing visual artifacts like flickering or incomplete images.

A critical aspect of display output is managing refresh rates. The refresh rate, measured in hertz (Hz), indicates how many times per second a display updates the image on screen. Standard refresh rates such as 60Hz, 120Hz, 144Hz, and even 240Hz are common today, with higher rates providing smoother and more responsive visual experiences. Especially in fast-paced games, higher refresh rates reduce motion blur and improve clarity, giving players a competitive edge.

However, if the GPU's frame rate doesn't match the display's refresh rate, issues like screen tearing can occur, where parts of multiple frames are displayed at once. Technologies like V-Sync attempt to mitigate this by synchronizing frame output with the monitor's refresh cycle, though they can sometimes introduce input lag. Adaptive synchronization technologies such as NVIDIA's G-Sync and AMD's FreeSync offer a more dynamic solution, adjusting the monitor's refresh rate to match the GPU's output in real-time. This not only eliminates tearing but also maintains smooth gameplay without the performance penalties associated with traditional V-Sync.

The process of rendering immersive, detailed virtual worlds is a marvel of modern engineering, blending advanced mathematics, physics, and artistic creativity into a seamless experience. From the early stages of vertex processing and rasterization to the cutting-edge techniques of ray tracing and path tracing, every part of the 3D graphics pipeline is meticulously optimized to deliver maximum performance and visual fidelity. With final output managed through frame buffers and synchronized with high-refresh-rate displays, today's graphics cards are capable of creating worlds so convincing that the line between reality and simulation continues to blur.

As GPUs continue to evolve, offering more power, better efficiency, and smarter rendering technologies, the future of interactive graphics promises even deeper immersion, richer details, and breathtaking realism. It's a testament to human ingenuity that billions of complex operations occur every second, all to create the magical, lifelike experiences that players, artists, and researchers around the world rely on every day.

The 3D Graphics Pipeline

Behind every breathtaking game world, every cinematic explosion, and every photorealistic environment lies an intricate process known as the 3D graphics pipeline. It's the invisible engine that transforms mathematical data into the rich, immersive worlds that captivate players and viewers alike.

Imagine standing at the edge of a vast, detailed landscape in a game. Trees sway in the wind, mountains stretch toward the sky, shadows dance realistically across the ground. All of that isn't just "drawn" onto your screen. It's calculated — a dynamic, complex flow of data moving through several distinct stages inside your graphics card.

The 3D graphics pipeline begins with model data—collections of vertices, edges, and faces that form the skeletons of digital objects. These data points define the shape and structure of every model, from the tiniest pebble to the grandest fortress. Once these basic frameworks are established, the pipeline applies transformations, rotating, scaling, and positioning objects correctly within a 3D space.

But geometry is only the beginning. The pipeline then enriches these shapes with layers of textures, colors, and lighting information, creating a surface that mimics reality—or fantasy—with stunning accuracy. Each stage is like a workshop, refining the raw materials into a finished masterpiece ready for the screen.

Without the pipeline, modern gaming and visualization as we know them simply wouldn't exist. It's the reason we can step into other worlds at the click of a button, experience lifelike simulations, and marvel at scenes that blur the line between the real and the virtual.

Vertex Processing, Rasterization, and Shading

Once the 3D models are prepared, they enter a series of transformational steps that are pivotal to how they appear on the screen — vertex processing, rasterization, and shading.

Vertex processing is where the raw geometry data is first manipulated. Vertices—essentially points in 3D space—are transformed from model space (their original coordinate system) into world space, then camera space, and finally into screen space. This series of transformations ensures that every object is correctly positioned from the viewer's perspective, taking into account camera angles, movement, and depth. During this phase, attributes like normals (which determine how light interacts with a surface) and texture coordinates are also calculated, setting the stage for realistic lighting and surface detail.

Next comes rasterization, one of the most vital—and fascinating—steps. Rasterization converts the processed 3D shapes into a 2D image. Since displays are made up of individual pixels, rasterization determines which pixels each triangle (the basic building block of 3D models) will cover. It's akin to painting a wireframe model onto a canvas, filling in the shapes with color and detail.

However, simply painting the shapes would yield flat, lifeless images. That's where shading steps in. Shading algorithms add depth, texture, and realism by simulating the interaction between light and surfaces. Whether it's the gentle gradation of a sunset on a character's armor or the harsh shadows in a gritty urban environment, shading breathes life into the image. Modern shading techniques can be incredibly sophisticated, accounting for reflections, refractions, subsurface scattering (like light through skin), and complex material properties that make virtual objects feel tangible.

Each of these processes is handled in real-time by specialized hardware units within the GPU, allowing scenes to be rendered at astonishing speeds and complexities unimaginable just a decade ago.

Real-Time Ray Tracing and Path Tracing

While traditional rendering methods have given us beautiful visuals, the pursuit of photorealism has led to groundbreaking innovations like real-time ray tracing and path tracing.

Ray tracing simulates the behavior of light in a highly realistic manner. In essence, it traces the path of light rays as they bounce around a scene, interacting with surfaces, reflecting off shiny materials, or refracting through transparent objects like glass or water. This method naturally produces incredibly realistic shadows, reflections, and lighting effects—subtleties that traditional rasterization methods often fake or approximate.

However, classic ray tracing was once considered far too computationally intensive for real-time applications like gaming. It was reserved for pre-rendered scenes in movies, where hours of rendering time per frame were acceptable. That changed dramatically with the advent of real-time ray tracing hardware acceleration (like NVIDIA's RTX technology), which introduced dedicated RT cores in GPUs. These specialized units handle the complex calculations necessary for ray tracing without sacrificing performance, making true-to-life lighting and reflections possible even during fast-paced gameplay.

Path tracing goes even further. It's a method where rays of light are randomly sampled many times per pixel, capturing even more detailed and accurate lighting effects. Path tracing can simulate phenomena like global illumination (light bouncing off surfaces multiple times) and caustics (light focusing through curved surfaces). It's more computationally demanding than ray tracing, but it's the gold standard for cinematic-quality rendering.

While full path tracing in real-time is still emerging technology, we're standing at the edge of a new frontier where even casual games can someday harness these techniques to blur the boundaries between virtual and real worlds.

Outputting to Displays: Frame Buffers and Refresh Rates

After all the heavy lifting inside the graphics card is complete, the final task is to output the rendered frame to the display. But even this seemingly simple step is a carefully managed process involving frame buffers and an understanding of refresh rates.

The frame buffer is a dedicated section of VRAM where the finished image is stored before being sent to your monitor. It acts as a staging area, ensuring that frames are complete and ready to display. The importance of a good frame buffer can't be overstated: without it, you'd experience tearing, flickering, and a host of visual artifacts that break immersion.

Modern GPUs often use techniques like triple buffering and adaptive sync technologies (such as G-Sync and FreeSync) to manage frame timing and synchronization with the display's refresh rate. This ensures smooth motion, reduces input lag, and prevents visual inconsistencies.

Refresh rate refers to how many times per second a display updates its image, measured in hertz (Hz). A 60Hz monitor refreshes the image 60 times per second, while gaming displays can reach 144Hz, 240Hz, or even higher. The GPU must output frames at a rate that matches or exceeds the monitor's refresh rate to deliver silky-smooth motion. If the GPU is too slow, you get stuttering; if it's too fast without sync mechanisms, you get tearing.

Chapter 4

Software Behind the Hardware

While the physical power of a graphics card captures the spotlight, it is the software behind the hardware that brings everything to life. From graphics APIs to drivers and firmware, the invisible layers of software ensure that GPUs perform at their best.

Graphics APIs (Application Programming Interfaces) serve as the bridge between a game or application and the GPU. Popular APIs like DirectX, Vulkan, OpenGL, and Metal allow developers to send commands to the GPU without worrying about its specific architecture. DirectX 12 provides deep access to hardware for optimized gaming on Windows, while Vulkan offers cross-platform, high-efficiency graphics control. OpenGL, although older, laid the foundation for 3D graphics programming, and Metal delivers streamlined performance on Apple devices. Each API plays a crucial role in maximizing graphical fidelity, efficiency, and platform compatibility.

However, APIs alone aren't enough. Drivers—software written by GPU manufacturers like NVIDIA, AMD, and Intel—translate API commands into machine-level instructions specific to each graphics card model. Drivers are critical for performance, fixing bugs, and introducing support for new features like ray tracing. Frequent driver updates ensure that new games run smoothly and that hardware continues to deliver optimal performance over time. For gamers and professionals alike, keeping drivers updated can mean the difference between a flawless experience and frustrating technical issues.

Beneath drivers lies another layer of control: the GPU's firmware. Stored directly on the graphics card, firmware (or VBIOS) defines how the GPU initializes, manages power, controls clock speeds, and handles thermal limits. Firmware updates can improve stability, unlock new features, or fine-tune performance. Some enthusiasts even flash custom firmware to overclock their GPUs for better performance, though this carries risks and is not generally recommended for casual users. Firmware also enables technologies like GPU Boost and Smart Access Memory, which automatically adjust performance based on real-time workloads and environmental conditions.

For developers, interacting with hardware happens through engines, APIs, and specialized tools. They use performance profilers, shader analyzers, and GPU debuggers to ensure their applications run efficiently across a range of hardware. Optimization choices—such as when to use lower-resolution textures or simplified lighting models—can greatly impact the end-user experience.

Meanwhile, gamers interact with GPU hardware more directly through graphics settings, control panels, and monitoring software. Adjusting resolution, texture quality, frame rate caps, and enabling or disabling advanced features like ray tracing are common ways gamers personalize their experience. Enthusiasts often take it further, overclocking their GPUs or fine-tuning fan curves to balance performance and thermals.

In short, while powerful hardware provides the foundation, it's the intricate and evolving layers of software that truly unleash a GPU's potential. Understanding the synergy between APIs, drivers, firmware, and user interaction is key to appreciating just how much work happens behind the scenes to render the worlds we see on our screens.

Graphics APIs: DirectX, Vulkan, OpenGL, and Metal

While powerful hardware drives the raw capability of a graphics card, it's the software layer—the graphics APIs—that truly unlocks that power and makes it accessible to games and applications.

A Graphics API (Application Programming Interface) acts as a translator between software and GPU hardware. Instead of programmers manually writing low-level instructions for every different type of GPU, they use APIs to issue high-level commands. These APIs standardize how tasks like drawing a triangle or applying a texture are communicated to the hardware.

One of the most widely used APIs is DirectX, particularly its latest versions like DirectX 12, developed by Microsoft. It offers powerful tools for managing graphics, audio, and input across Windows systems and Xbox consoles. DirectX 12 introduced major advances in low-level hardware access, allowing developers to squeeze every bit of performance from the GPU while managing multiple tasks (like rendering, physics, and AI) more efficiently.

OpenGL—short for Open Graphics Library—was historically one of the first major cross-platform graphics APIs. It provided a standard that worked across Windows, macOS, and Linux, making it a favorite among developers needing broad compatibility. Although newer technologies have somewhat surpassed it in cutting-edge capabilities, OpenGL's influence on modern graphics programming is undeniable.

Then there's Vulkan, the modern successor to OpenGL, designed to offer even closer-to-the-metal control over GPU resources. Vulkan enables better multithreading, lower CPU overhead, and higher efficiency, making it ideal for demanding applications like AAA games, VR experiences, and simulation software. Its cross-platform nature also makes it popular among Android game developers.

For Apple devices, Metal serves as the native graphics API, providing a streamlined and highly efficient pathway between apps and Apple's GPUs. Metal's design philosophy emphasizes minimal overhead and maximized performance, helping developers achieve console-quality graphics on iPhones, iPads, and Macs.

Choosing the right API can dramatically influence performance, graphical fidelity, and compatibility. For developers, it's not just about building a game—it's about ensuring the game runs optimally across a sea of different hardware setups.

The Role of Drivers in Performance and Compatibility

While graphics APIs set the rules of communication, drivers are the crucial interpreters that ensure everything functions correctly. A driver is specialized software written by GPU manufacturers like NVIDIA, AMD, or Intel, designed to interface between the operating system, the graphics API, and the specific GPU hardware.

Drivers perform a staggering number of tasks behind the scenes. They translate the commands from APIs into the exact machine-level instructions the GPU can understand. They optimize performance by fine-tuning how different hardware resources are allocated during rendering. They manage memory, synchronize parallel operations across thousands of GPU cores, and even handle error recovery if something goes wrong.

Keeping drivers updated is vital for performance and compatibility. New driver versions often introduce performance improvements for the latest games, fix bugs that cause crashes or graphical glitches, and add support for new features like ray tracing or DLSS (Deep Learning Super Sampling).

However, drivers are incredibly complex, and small flaws can create major problems. That's why rigorous testing across a wide variety of hardware and software configurations is essential before a driver is released publicly.

For end-users—whether gamers, creative professionals, or everyday PC users—understanding the importance of drivers means fewer headaches, better system stability, and an overall smoother experience.

Firmware and GPU Optimization

Beneath the operating system and drivers lies another crucial layer: firmware. Think of firmware as the embedded operating system that lives inside the GPU itself, stored in non-volatile memory on the graphics card.

GPU firmware, often referred to as the VBIOS (Video BIOS), controls the most fundamental aspects of how the card operates. It defines power limits, temperature thresholds, fan speeds, memory timings, and clock speeds. When you power on your computer, the GPU firmware initializes the card and prepares it for communication with the CPU and operating system.

Manufacturers frequently update GPU firmware to fix bugs, improve stability, or unlock new performance features. Enthusiasts sometimes flash custom firmware to overclock their GPUs beyond factory settings, though this carries risk and can void warranties.

Modern GPUs also feature built-in optimization technologies driven by firmware. Examples include NVIDIA's GPU Boost or AMD's Smart Access Memory, which dynamically adjust performance characteristics based on workload, thermal conditions, and available power headroom. These optimizations ensure that users get the maximum performance possible without having to manually tweak settings.

In essence, firmware acts as the hidden mastermind, orchestrating how the GPU behaves at the most granular level, ensuring it performs optimally and safely under a wide range of conditions.

How Developers and Gamers Interact with the Hardware

At the highest level, the software and hardware synergy culminates in how developers and gamers actually experience and utilize the graphics card.

For developers, interaction with hardware largely happens through APIs, engines, and debugging tools. Game engines like Unreal Engine and Unity abstract away much of the low-level complexity, allowing developers to focus on crafting content rather than managing every individual draw call. However, developers must still think carefully about optimization—deciding when to use high-polygon models, how to manage texture streaming, and when to enable advanced effects like ambient occlusion or real-time reflections.

GPU profiling tools, provided by companies like NVIDIA (Nsight) and AMD (Radeon GPU

Profiler), allow developers to dive deep into performance analysis. They can see where bottlenecks occur, optimize shaders, balance CPU-GPU workloads, and fine-tune every frame rendered by the engine.

For gamers, interaction with the GPU tends to be a bit more hands-on—through graphics settings in games, driver management, and system tweaks. Gamers adjust options like texture quality, resolution, frame rate caps, and post-processing effects to achieve their desired balance between performance and visual fidelity.

Power users and enthusiasts go even deeper, using utilities like MSI Afterburner or AMD Radeon Software to monitor GPU temperatures, overclock performance, or undervolt their cards for better efficiency. Understanding how to tweak settings to get the best experience from a graphics card is part of the culture of PC gaming itself.

Whether building breathtaking worlds, analyzing performance down to the last millisecond, or simply tuning a system for buttery-smooth gameplay, the relationship between developers, gamers, and GPU hardware is one of constant discovery, experimentation, and innovation.

Chapter 5

Powering Gaming and Real-Time Visualization

Gaming today is a world of hyper-realistic visuals, cinematic storytelling, and immersive environments that react dynamically to every player decision. But behind the smooth animations and jaw-dropping visual effects lies an incredible engine of computational power: the modern graphics card. Far from being a mere add-on, the GPU has become the cornerstone of modern gaming and real-time visualization, acting as both the muscle and mind of the visual experience. Whether it's navigating richly detailed open worlds, participating in massive multiplayer battles, or experiencing breathtaking simulations, the graphics card is what makes it all come alive.

As the demands of players grow, so does the complexity of what a graphics card must deliver. Today's titles are no longer just pixelated distractions; they are living, breathing ecosystems that push the boundaries of visual fidelity, physics simulations, artificial intelligence, and real-time responsiveness. Each frame you see is the result of thousands of calculations executed in milliseconds—textures rendered, shadows cast, reflections simulated—all stitched together into a seamless experience.

What makes a game feel smooth? What transforms it from a flat digital landscape into a vibrant world you can almost touch? The answers lie in how the GPU handles lighting, motion, detail, and timing. This chapter unpacks how graphics cards meet the insatiable hunger of modern visual media—from games pushing the frontier of realism, to technologies like Virtual and Augmented Reality that redefine the meaning of immersion. For buyers, understanding what drives these visuals is essential to making the right investment in their gaming or visualization rig.

The Demands of Modern Games

Today's games are technical marvels, combining storytelling, artificial intelligence, physics, and rendering into a synchronized dance. The complexity involved in just displaying a single frame of gameplay would have been unimaginable a decade ago. But modern games aren't content with looking good—they demand high frame rates, low latency, and real-time responsiveness, all at ultra-high resolutions.

Graphics cards now have to process increasingly large textures, simulate lifelike lighting and shadows, render thousands of objects on screen, and do it all in real-time without dropping frames. A single AAA title might contain gigabytes of textures, complex particle systems for weather effects, destructible environments, and dynamic lighting that shifts with time of day. The card must juggle all these elements, making split-second decisions while maintaining high performance.

A demanding game like Cyberpunk 2077 or Red Dead Redemption 2 can utilize every ounce of GPU power available, especially when played at 4K resolution. The game engine sends instructions to the GPU to compute geometry, shading, occlusion, and post-processing effects like motion blur and ambient occlusion.

Meanwhile, AI-driven behaviors, physics simulations, and particle effects layer on even more complexity.

Players expect responsiveness and beauty in equal measure. A game must not only look stunning, but it must feel fluid. A lag of even 50 milliseconds can ruin a competitive match or break immersion in a narrative-driven experience. That's why graphics cards are designed with not only power but efficiency in mind—squeezing every frame out in the shortest time possible.

Game developers are acutely aware of these GPU capabilities. Studios build engines around specific GPU features, such as NVIDIA's DLSS (Deep Learning Super Sampling) or AMD's FidelityFX Super Resolution, to optimize how frames are rendered. These tools help maintain visual fidelity without sacrificing performance, making the most of available hardware.

As games continue evolving with AI-driven NPCs, destructible environments, and cinematic storytelling, the demands on graphics hardware will only escalate. A future-proof GPU is more than a luxury—it's a necessity for anyone serious about gaming or real-time visualization.

Achieving Realistic Lighting, Shadows, and Physics

The realism in modern games hinges on how accurately light, shadow, and physical interactions are rendered. From the soft diffusion of sunlight through leaves to the sharp shadows of a flickering flame, lighting is what gives virtual worlds their soul. Graphics cards are now built with dedicated hardware and algorithms to simulate these visual effects with astonishing fidelity.

Lighting is not just about brightness; it's about how light interacts with every surface it touches. The GPU calculates reflections, refractions, subsurface scattering, and light bounces—all in real-time. Technologies like real-time global illumination and screen space reflections ensure that light behaves as it would in the physical world. A stone wall doesn't just look grey; it absorbs some light, reflects others, and subtly changes based on time of day or light source movement.

Shadows, often overlooked, are equally essential for realism. Soft shadows, hard shadows, dynamic shadows—all contribute to the depth and immersion of a scene. GPUs calculate shadow maps and use advanced algorithms to render these shadows accurately, even as the light source or object moves. Cascaded shadow maps and contact-hardening shadows help create depth and realism, particularly in large outdoor environments.

Then there's physics—the invisible hand that governs how objects move, fall, and interact. A believable world must obey the laws of gravity, friction, and collision. When a building collapses or a character stumbles, the GPU processes rigid body dynamics, particle physics, and fluid simulations to ensure these interactions feel authentic.

High-end GPUs are now designed with dedicated hardware acceleration for ray tracing, which brings lighting and shadows to the next level. Ray tracing mimics the path of individual photons, simulating the way they bounce off surfaces, scatter in fog, or get absorbed. It's computationally intensive, but when done well, it can blur the line between real and virtual.

Developers rely on APIs and engines that can offload these tasks to the GPU efficiently. Technologies like NVIDIA RTX and AMD Ray Accelerators are purpose-built to handle ray tracing without a performance crash. As hardware continues evolving, real-time path tracing—considered the holy grail of lighting realism—is becoming increasingly viable.

From the glint of armor in the sun to the way fog rolls over a swamp at dusk, every visual nuance relies on the GPU's ability to simulate real-world physics. For gamers and creators alike, the result is not just a beautiful scene, but a world that breathes, reacts, and feels alive.

4K, High Frame Rates, and Adaptive Sync Technologies

Gaming used to be a race toward more pixels. Now, it's a careful balance of resolution, frame rate, and synchronization. As 4K monitors and displays become mainstream, graphics cards must handle four times the pixel load of standard 1080p—without compromising performance.

4K resolution delivers unparalleled detail. Textures become razor-sharp, distant objects remain crisp, and environments feel more lifelike. But rendering at 4K requires enormous memory bandwidth, GPU core performance, and optimized pipelines. Cards with higher VRAM capacities and wider memory buses excel in this area, allowing for large texture buffers and quick data transfer.

However, resolution alone isn't the full story. Frame rate—measured in frames per second (FPS)—is just as crucial. Competitive gamers often prioritize 120Hz or 240Hz refresh rates over sheer resolution, seeking the fastest possible response time. The smoother the frame delivery, the more immediate and tactile the gameplay feels.

Adaptive Sync technologies like NVIDIA G-SYNC and AMD FreeSync help bridge the gap between a display's refresh rate and the GPU's output. Without them, mismatches cause screen tearing—visual artifacts that break immersion. With Adaptive Sync, the display refreshes only when a new frame is ready, ensuring a seamless visual flow.

Modern GPUs include technologies like variable rate shading and DLSS to optimize how frames are rendered. Variable rate shading allows the GPU to prioritize rendering resources where they're needed most—like the center of the screen—while lowering detail in peripheral areas. This maintains performance without noticeable quality loss.

Deep Learning Super Sampling, or DLSS, is another game-changer. It uses AI models to render games at lower resolutions and then upscale them intelligently, preserving sharpness and detail. DLSS 3 takes it a step further by generating entire intermediate frames, boosting FPS without demanding extra GPU power.

With support for HDMI 2.1 and DisplayPort 2.0, high-end GPUs can now push 4K at 120Hz and even 8K resolutions in certain conditions. These features are critical for gamers who want the ultimate visual experience or professionals working in detailed simulation environments.

When shopping for a graphics card, understanding how it handles these technologies helps buyers make the right investment. It's not just about peak performance; it's about consistency, adaptability, and future-proofing.

Graphics Cards in VR, AR, and High-End Simulations

Virtual Reality and Augmented Reality have transformed how we interact with digital content. Unlike traditional displays, VR and AR immerse the user within the environment, demanding real-time responsiveness and incredibly low latency. Graphics cards must deliver frames at blazing speeds—often 90 FPS or more—to avoid motion sickness and maintain immersion.

In VR, every movement of your head, hand, or eyes needs to be reflected instantly within the virtual world. This requires GPUs to render two separate views simultaneously—one for each eye—at high resolution and low latency. Techniques like foveated rendering help by reducing detail in peripheral vision and concentrating resources on where the eye is focused.

Augmented Reality adds digital elements to the physical world. Whether it's a digital assistant guiding a technician or a game overlaid on real-world terrain, AR places unique demands on the GPU. It must process camera input, map the environment in real-time, and integrate 3D elements without lag.

Simulations—whether for aerospace, architecture, medical training, or automotive development—rely heavily on real-time rendering. Here, the GPU is used not for entertainment but precision. Flight simulators must calculate aerodynamics, physics, and environmental visuals in real-time. Medical trainers depend on lifelike anatomy rendered in full detail. Architectural walk-throughs visualize how light interacts with materials before a single brick is laid.

Professional-grade GPUs, like NVIDIA's RTX A-series or AMD's Radeon PRO cards, are optimized for these tasks. They support massive frame buffers, ECC memory, and certified drivers for stability under demanding applications. Ray tracing, AI denoising, and high-speed simulation rendering allow engineers and designers to iterate faster and more accurately.

For buyers interested in VR, AR, or simulation work, choosing a graphics card isn't just about gaming performance. It's about how well the card handles latency, resolution scaling, motion tracking, and sustained workloads. The right GPU transforms a simple headset or simulation suite into a powerful tool for exploration, training, and creation.

From casual gamers to professionals, the role of the graphics card has expanded far beyond pixels on a screen. It powers immersive experiences, enhances realism, and opens doors to entirely new digital frontiers.

Chapter 6

GPUs Beyond Gaming: The Rise of AI

Graphics cards have long been associated with immersive gameplay, stunning visual effects, and ultra-high frame rates. But in recent years, GPUs have quietly evolved into a driving force behind some of the most advanced technological frontiers. From powering deep learning models that mimic human reasoning to enabling real-time analysis in autonomous vehicles, the modern GPU is no longer just a gaming powerhouse—it's a computational engine fueling the future.

Buyers entering the GPU market today are often drawn by raw performance metrics relevant to gaming. However, the discerning buyer who also considers productivity, creative workloads, or future applications like AI should look at a GPU not only as a piece of gaming hardware but as a versatile computing tool. This shift is increasingly important as industries such as healthcare, robotics, finance, and scientific research lean heavily on parallel processing and GPU-accelerated systems. The story of the modern GPU is one of transformation—from a tool designed for pixels to a core component of the AI revolution.

Why GPUs Excel at AI and Machine Learning

Traditional CPUs were designed for sequential task execution, meaning they excel at tasks that require strong single-thread performance. GPUs, on the other hand, are built with thousands of smaller cores that can handle many operations simultaneously. This design is perfect for the matrix operations and vector computations central to machine learning and artificial intelligence.

The strength of a GPU lies in its parallel processing capability. When training a deep neural network, millions of weights and biases must be adjusted simultaneously over countless iterations. This computational load is easily distributed across the multiple cores of a GPU, allowing for significant speedups compared to CPU-only systems. Tasks that used to take days or weeks on CPUs can now be performed in hours or minutes using a GPU.

Furthermore, GPUs maintain high memory bandwidth and specialized compute instructions optimized for AI workloads. The ability to swiftly move large datasets between memory and processing units allows machine learning models to scale effectively without bottlenecks. AI research is often limited by time-to-iteration, and GPUs enable much faster iteration cycles, fostering rapid development and innovation.

Organizations from startups to tech giants have adopted GPUs as their go-to tool for AI. Whether you're building a smart personal assistant, developing real-time translation software, or creating recommendation systems, a powerful GPU can drastically reduce training times and improve inference performance.

Tensor Cores, Parallelism, and Deep Learning

The introduction of tensor cores in NVIDIA's Volta architecture marked a turning point for AI acceleration. Unlike traditional CUDA cores, tensor cores are specialized for deep learning operations, particularly for matrix multiplication and accumulation, which are foundational in neural network training. By processing these calculations at a much faster rate, tensor cores enhance throughput and lower latency for AI tasks.

Tensor cores support mixed-precision computing, using formats like FP16 and INT8 in addition to standard FP32. This allows developers to run AI models faster and with reduced power consumption, without compromising accuracy. The result is significantly more efficient deep learning processing—especially valuable for tasks like real-time object detection, natural language processing, and video analytics.

Parallelism in GPUs takes center stage when it comes to training large-scale deep learning models. Each layer of a neural network can contain millions of parameters. During forward and backward propagation, the workload can be divided into smaller tasks that are processed in tandem by hundreds or thousands of GPU cores. This design drastically accelerates both training and inference.

As AI frameworks like TensorFlow and PyTorch have matured, they've integrated optimized libraries that take full advantage of GPU architecture. These include cuDNN (CUDA Deep Neural Network library), which provides highly tuned implementations for standard routines like convolutions and activation functions. Developers can now harness the full power of tensor cores and parallel GPU threads with just a few lines of code.

Real-World Applications: Autonomous Vehicles, Robotics, Healthcare

What once sounded like science fiction—self-driving cars, robot surgeons, real-time disease diagnostics—is rapidly becoming reality, thanks in large part to GPUs. These use cases illustrate just how deeply embedded graphics processors have become in modern innovation.

Autonomous vehicles, for example, rely on GPUs to process vast amounts of visual and sensor data in real time. Cameras, LiDAR systems, GPS modules, and radar constantly feed data into the vehicle's onboard systems. A GPU rapidly analyzes this data, identifying road signs, lane markings, pedestrians, and other vehicles—all while making split-second decisions to ensure passenger safety.

In robotics, GPUs enable real-time control, motion planning, and environmental perception. Robots in manufacturing use AI models to adjust their tasks dynamically, identifying defects, adapting to changing components, or responding to human interaction. High-throughput GPU processing allows these decisions to happen with minimal latency, increasing efficiency and productivity.

Healthcare has seen remarkable GPU-driven breakthroughs. From accelerating MRI scan reconstructions to training models that detect tumors in radiology images, GPUs are being leveraged to enhance diagnostics, treatment planning, and patient outcomes. AI algorithms powered by GPUs can analyze millions of medical records, images, and genomic sequences to offer insights that would take humans years to uncover.

Even during global health crises, GPUs have been vital. During the COVID-19 pandemic, researchers used GPU-accelerated simulations to model the spread of the virus and screen potential treatments. As medical data continues to grow exponentially, GPU-accelerated platforms ensure that innovation keeps pace.

CUDA, OpenCL, and Other Computing Frameworks

To fully leverage the computing power of GPUs, developers turn to programming frameworks designed specifically for general-purpose computing on graphics processors (GPGPU). CUDA, developed by NVIDIA, is the most popular and powerful of these platforms. It allows developers to write highly parallelized code that executes directly on NVIDIA GPUs.

CUDA gives developers low-level access to the GPU's hardware, enabling them to fine-tune performance for specific applications. Libraries like cuBLAS (for linear algebra), cuFFT (for fast Fourier transforms), and Thrust (for parallel algorithms) extend CUDA's capabilities, allowing researchers and engineers to create complex GPU-accelerated applications without reinventing the wheel.

OpenCL (Open Computing Language), in contrast, is a cross-platform framework that supports a wide variety of devices, including

GPUs from AMD, Intel, and others. Though typically not as optimized as CUDA for NVIDIA hardware, OpenCL provides flexibility in heterogeneous environments where multiple vendors' hardware is used together.

Other frameworks such as ROCm (Radeon Open Compute) for AMD GPUs, and SYCL (from the Khronos Group), continue to gain traction. Meanwhile, high-level machine learning frameworks—TensorFlow, PyTorch, and MXNet—offer abstracted APIs that compile down to CUDA or OpenCL under the hood, making it easier for developers to create GPU-accelerated applications without deep hardware knowledge.

These frameworks are the bridge between hardware and innovation. They empower developers to use GPUs not only for rendering graphics but to solve some of the world's toughest computational challenges—quickly, efficiently, and at scale.

Chapter 7

Behind the Scenes: How Graphics Cards Are Made

Graphics cards have become the lifeblood of modern digital experiences, whether it's gaming, high-performance computing, artificial intelligence, or real-time 3D rendering. For many consumers, the experience begins at the point of purchase—unboxing a sleek, powerful piece of hardware. But behind every GPU lies a complex and often unseen world of innovation, precision engineering, and global logistics. From intricate silicon architecture to rigorous quality control and final packaging, the journey of a graphics card is a testament to advanced manufacturing and design. Understanding how these components come to life can offer buyers a new appreciation for what goes into powering their favorite games or professional applications.

Designing the Silicon: Architecture and Fabrication

At the heart of every graphics card lies the silicon chip, an incredibly dense and complex piece of engineering that serves as the GPU's brain. Designing this chip begins years before it ever reaches a factory, often involving thousands of engineers working across disciplines—hardware design, thermal engineering, memory architecture, and more.

Architects start by defining what the next generation of GPUs should achieve. Do they need to prioritize raw power for gaming? Efficiency for laptops? Or specialized cores for AI and scientific computation? Once the purpose is clear, the architecture is mapped out using extremely sophisticated design tools. These tools create a layout of billions of transistors arranged in nanoscale formations that determine how information is processed, rendered, or accelerated.

Once the design is finalized, it's sent to fabrication facilities—known as foundries. Companies like TSMC and Samsung are the industry's leaders, using advanced lithography machines to etch those complex designs onto silicon wafers. This is done using ultraviolet light and chemical treatments in a process called photolithography. At this scale, even a single speck of dust can ruin an entire wafer, so fabrication takes place in sterile cleanrooms that are hundreds of times cleaner than a hospital operating theater.

Modern GPUs often use process nodes such as 5nm or 3nm, which refers to the size of the transistors. Smaller transistors mean more of them can fit into the same space, increasing performance and reducing power consumption. However, moving to smaller nodes increases complexity and cost, making the design and fabrication stages some of the most expensive in the entire GPU lifecycle.

Manufacturing, Assembly, and Quality Control

Once the silicon wafers are completed, each wafer is cut into tiny individual chips, known as dies. These dies are rigorously tested for defects—only those that meet high-performance standards are kept. The good dies are then packaged into a structure that includes heat spreaders, connection pins, and protective housing. This process is known as packaging, and it prepares the chip to be mounted onto a graphics card.

The next step is assembling the graphics card itself. A PCB (Printed Circuit Board) is designed to house not only the GPU chip but also memory modules, voltage regulation modules (VRMs), and various input/output components like HDMI or DisplayPort connectors. Robotic arms and precision soldering machines place each component in exact positions on the board, with margins of error measured in microns.

Following assembly, each card goes through an array of quality control procedures. These include thermal stress tests, power draw measurements, and performance benchmarking. Cards are placed in temperature chambers and run under load to simulate real-world usage. If a card fails to meet benchmarks or exhibits instability, it is either discarded or sent for rework.

Manufacturers often over-engineer their cooling solutions to accommodate high thermal output while maintaining silent operation. Fans, heatsinks, and sometimes even liquid cooling blocks are integrated to ensure thermal management. The finished product is then enclosed in a carefully designed shroud that enhances both function and aesthetics.

From Foundries to Finished Products

The logistics behind moving GPUs from production lines to store shelves involve a global supply chain that rivals any consumer product. After final assembly, GPUs are packaged for shipment in anti-static bags and cushioned boxes. These are then loaded into crates and transported to distributors and retailers across the world.

Customs clearance, freight handling, and inventory management are crucial steps in this process. Delays at any point can cause ripple effects across the entire tech industry, particularly during periods of high demand like holiday seasons or new product launches.

Retail units are then either sent to brick-and-mortar stores or e-commerce hubs. In many cases, third-party vendors such as ASUS, MSI, and Gigabyte will add their own branding, cooler designs, and custom PCBs before repackaging the GPU for the consumer market. These third-party models often vary in terms of cooling efficiency, factory overclocking, and aesthetics.

Each step from foundry to final sale is meticulously timed and monitored to ensure consistency. Any lapse in quality or shipment reliability can lead to recalls, reputational damage, or even financial loss. For consumers, the end result may appear seamless, but behind the scenes, it's a ballet of engineering, logistics, and business coordination.

Major Players: NVIDIA, AMD, Intel, and Others

The graphics card market is dominated by a few major players, each with its own philosophy and design focus. NVIDIA, for example, has long been a leader in gaming and professional graphics. Its GeForce line caters to gamers, while the Quadro and RTX A-series are aimed at creative professionals and enterprise users. NVIDIA has also been instrumental in pushing AI computing through its CUDA architecture and data center-focused GPUs like the A100 and H100.

AMD, on the other hand, has been gaining ground rapidly. Its Radeon series competes directly with NVIDIA's GeForce cards, offering competitive pricing and performance. AMD's strength lies in its integration of CPU and GPU technology, which provides synergy across its Ryzen and Radeon platforms. Technologies like Smart Access Memory and FidelityFX are examples of AMD's holistic ecosystem approach.

Intel, a newcomer in the discrete GPU space, has introduced the Intel Arc series. Although it's early days for Intel's GPU division, the company brings decades of silicon expertise and a massive R&D budget. With time, Intel is likely to become a significant player, especially in entry-level and mid-range segments.

Beyond the big three, companies like Apple have begun designing their own GPUs for specific applications, especially in mobile and desktop computing. Startups and niche manufacturers are also entering the field, focusing on custom chips for AI, blockchain, or other specialized workloads.

For the buyer, understanding who makes the GPU and how it's made offers a valuable perspective on price, performance, and longevity. Each manufacturer brings something different to the table, and knowing the journey from architecture to shelf can empower smarter, more informed purchasing decisions.

Chapter 8

Tuning, Overclocking, and Emerging Technologies

Modern graphics cards aren't just tools for displaying visuals—they're powerhouses capable of dynamic performance adjustments, customization, and innovation. As demand for greater speed, visual fidelity, and efficiency grows, users increasingly look for ways to get the most out of their GPUs. Whether it's tuning performance through overclocking or staying informed on revolutionary advancements like AI upscaling and virtual GPUs, understanding these facets empowers both gamers and professionals. With the industry also leaning into sustainability and energy efficiency, the landscape of graphics technology is being reshaped at a rapid pace.

Overclocking for Performance Gains

Overclocking is the practice of pushing a graphics card beyond its factory-set performance limits. This means increasing the GPU's core clock speed and memory clock rate to gain higher frame rates, better responsiveness, and smoother overall gameplay or productivity performance. For many users, overclocking offers a budget-friendly way to boost output without needing to upgrade their hardware.

A graphics card's clock speed determines how fast it processes data, and manufacturers often leave a bit of "headroom"—a margin where the GPU can safely operate at higher frequencies. Enthusiasts take advantage of this by using software tools such as MSI Afterburner, EVGA Precision X1, or AMD's Radeon Software to manually tweak these settings. Through trial and error, they identify the GPU's performance ceiling while keeping temperatures and power draw within safe boundaries.

However, overclocking isn't as simple as sliding a bar to the right. Stability testing is essential, as pushing a GPU too far can lead to crashes, artifacts on screen, or even hardware degradation. Benchmarking software like 3DMark, Unigine Heaven, and FurMark help test stability under load, while monitoring tools track temperatures, voltage, and fan speeds. Balancing performance gains with long-term reliability becomes a central goal.

Many modern graphics cards now come with factory overclocked (OC) models, where manufacturers have already tuned them for higher performance within tested limits. These offer peace of mind with enhanced output straight out of the box, but custom tuning still allows enthusiasts to squeeze out even more performance based on their system setup and cooling capabilities.

Cooling Strategies for Overclockers

When a GPU runs faster, it naturally generates more heat. Keeping it cool becomes a top priority, especially during overclocking sessions where sustained high performance is expected. The effectiveness of cooling determines not only system stability but also how far a user can push their hardware.

Air cooling remains the most common solution for consumer graphics cards. High-quality aftermarket air coolers feature large heatsinks, multiple heat pipes, and dual or triple-fan configurations to dissipate heat effectively. Cards from brands like ASUS ROG, Gigabyte AORUS, and MSI Gaming X often employ advanced fan curves, thermal pads, and custom PCB layouts to improve airflow and heat transfer.

For those seeking superior thermal performance, liquid cooling provides a more efficient alternative. All-in-one (AIO) GPU coolers and custom water blocks allow users to circulate coolant across the GPU die, transferring heat to a radiator where it is dispersed by fans. These setups can dramatically reduce temperatures, enabling higher and more stable overclocks. However, they require more space, cost, and maintenance.

Innovative solutions like hybrid cooling (combining air and liquid), vapor chambers, and graphene-based thermal pads are also gaining traction. These methods aim to strike a balance between cost, complexity, and cooling performance.

Overclockers often complement their GPU cooling with optimized airflow within the PC case. Ensuring that intake and exhaust fans are properly aligned, cleaning dust filters, and using thermal monitoring software ensures that the system maintains ideal conditions under load.

Trends Shaping the Future: AI Upscaling, Cloud Gaming, Virtual GPUs

The graphics card industry is rapidly evolving, not just through faster chips but also via paradigm-shifting technologies. AI upscaling, cloud-based rendering, and virtualization are at the forefront of a new era in how graphics power is delivered and consumed.

AI upscaling, notably championed by NVIDIA's Deep Learning Super Sampling (DLSS) and AMD's FidelityFX Super Resolution (FSR), uses neural networks to render lower-resolution frames and intelligently upscale them to higher resolutions. This provides significant performance gains while maintaining visual fidelity, making 4K gaming viable even on mid-tier hardware. By training models to predict how pixels should appear, these technologies reduce the workload on GPUs while delivering crisp visuals.

Cloud gaming is another groundbreaking trend. Platforms like NVIDIA GeForce NOW, Xbox Cloud Gaming, and Google Stadia allow users to stream high-fidelity games over the internet without needing a powerful local GPU. Instead, powerful data center GPUs render the games remotely and transmit the output in real time. This approach democratizes access to premium gaming experiences, though it requires low-latency, high-bandwidth connections to function seamlessly.

Virtual GPUs (vGPUs) are also transforming industries beyond gaming. In professional settings like virtual desktop infrastructure (VDI), architecture, and scientific research, vGPUs allow multiple users to share the power of a single GPU. Enterprises can deploy scalable computing environments where heavy

3D workloads or AI computations are offloaded to centralized GPU clusters, increasing flexibility and reducing hardware costs.

These technologies highlight a shift from raw hardware performance to smarter, distributed, and more efficient solutions that adapt to user needs and global connectivity.

Green Computing and the Push for Energy-Efficient GPUs

As GPUs become more powerful, their energy consumption has also grown—a concern in both environmental and operational contexts. The shift toward green computing seeks to create GPUs that deliver outstanding performance while minimizing their carbon footprint and energy demands.

Manufacturers are now prioritizing performance-per-watt metrics, a key indicator of efficiency. NVIDIA's Ampere and Ada Lovelace architectures, for example, make significant strides in delivering more frames per watt compared to previous generations.

Similarly, AMD's RDNA and RDNA 2 architectures emphasize energy optimization by refining compute unit design, memory handling, and workload distribution.

Smaller manufacturing nodes—like TSMC's 5nm process—play a pivotal role in reducing power consumption. These allow for more transistors in a compact area, enabling faster processing with lower energy requirements. Additionally, adaptive power scaling techniques, where the GPU intelligently reduces voltage and frequency during lighter workloads, help conserve energy without compromising user experience.

In the consumer space, features like NVIDIA's WhisperMode and AMD's Radeon Chill actively manage frame rates and fan speeds to balance performance and power usage. These options are increasingly appreciated by gamers using laptops or compact builds where thermal and acoustic efficiency matter.

The industry is also witnessing a rise in environmental commitments. Major companies are investing in carbon-neutral production, recyclable materials, and energy-efficient packaging. Data centers supporting cloud gaming or AI training with GPUs are adopting green energy sources and optimizing cooling systems to reduce overall emissions.

As sustainability becomes a global imperative, energy-efficient GPUs not only address environmental concerns but also offer economic benefits. Lower energy bills, longer hardware life, and quieter operation make efficient GPUs a smart choice for users who want power without compromise.

Chapter 9

Choosing and Investing in the Right Graphics Card

Choosing the right graphics card can feel like stepping into a maze of model numbers, technical jargon, and marketing claims. For the average buyer—and even for many tech-savvy users—the sheer volume of available options, coupled with the rapid pace at which new GPUs hit the market, can make the decision overwhelming. Whether you're building your dream gaming PC, setting up a workstation for AI research, or just seeking smoother visuals for everyday computing, the right GPU is not a one-size-fits-all answer. It requires understanding your goals, budget, and how the specs on the box translate into real-world performance.

Graphics cards today aren't just about raw power. They represent a balance between performance, thermal management, power consumption, and future compatibility. One card might deliver unmatched frame rates in ultra-high settings but require a larger case and robust cooling setup. Another may be optimized for AI computation, making it ideal for machine learning tasks but overkill for gaming. There's also the consideration of brand features—NVIDIA's DLSS, AMD's FSR, ray tracing performance, driver stability, and software ecosystems can all influence the overall user experience. Even the physical size of the card—its length, number of fans, and thickness—can determine whether it will fit in your case.

Making the right decision is not just about avoiding buyer's remorse. It's an investment in future productivity or enjoyment, and sometimes both. Graphics cards often represent one of the most expensive components in a PC build, so it's critical that your money goes toward features and capabilities that matter to your specific use case. Gamers want high frame rates and support for the latest graphical features. AI practitioners need deep learning acceleration and memory bandwidth. Professional users might need certifications for applications like CAD or video editing software. Even casual users have concerns—noise levels, heat output, and energy efficiency can all become important considerations over time.

And let's not ignore the market itself. Prices fluctuate due to factors like supply chain issues, crypto mining demand, and generational product launches. Investing in a GPU isn't just about the card's capabilities on paper, but also about timing your purchase, understanding depreciation, and knowing how long your investment will stay relevant. Pair that with the rising popularity of used GPUs, warranties, and performance per dollar considerations, and suddenly the shopping process becomes part research, part strategy.

This chapter provides a practical guide to navigating the noise. From understanding what specs truly matter, to aligning your choice with your goals, budgeting wisely, and thinking ahead to what's next—we'll explore how to make a smart, future-ready investment in one of the most important pieces of modern computing hardware.

Decoding Specifications: What Really Matters

Walk into any electronics store or scroll through an online retailer, and you're instantly met with rows of graphics cards, each plastered with a matrix of specs—VRAM, core clocks, boost clocks, CUDA cores, shader units, memory bandwidth, TDP, PCIe interface, and more. It's easy to be dazzled or overwhelmed. For many buyers, the natural impulse is to gravitate toward the card with the largest number or the flashiest description. But in reality, not every specification holds the same weight, and the key to making an informed purchase lies in understanding what each of these terms means in practice—and, more importantly, how it affects your experience.

Let's start with the specification that gets the most attention: Video RAM (VRAM). VRAM functions like the short-term memory of your GPU. It temporarily stores textures, lighting maps, shaders, and other assets that the graphics processor needs to access quickly. For gaming at 1080p, 6GB to 8GB of VRAM is usually sufficient. Move up to 1440p or 4K gaming, or start running more demanding titles or mods, and you'll see clear benefits from 10GB or more. For creative professionals—especially video editors, 3D artists, or AI researchers—VRAM becomes even more important. Large datasets, high-resolution frames, or complex 3D scenes require more VRAM to process efficiently without bottlenecks.

Clock speeds are another common talking point, often separated into "base clock" and "boost clock." These values represent how fast the GPU core operates, usually measured in MHz or GHz. While it's tempting to think that higher numbersautomatically mean better performance, the reality is more nuanced. Clock speeds alone don't determine how powerful a graphics card is. A card's efficiency in utilizing its clock speed—how well it maintains that speed under pressure, and how it works in tandem with other components like cooling systems and power delivery—plays a much bigger role in actual performance. Some GPUs with slightly lower boost clocks can outperform higher-clocked rivals simply because they're built on a more efficient architecture or maintain stable frequencies during sustained workloads.

Moving beyond clock speed, we arrive at shader units, CUDA cores, or stream processors—the specific term depends on whether you're looking at NVIDIA, AMD, or Intel cards. These cores are essentially the workforce of the GPU, handling rendering, shading,lighting calculations, and a variety of parallel processing tasks that define how quickly and efficiently your card can manage graphical data. When evaluating shader units or core counts, many users fall into the trap of thinking that a higher number automatically guarantees superior performance. But just like clock speed, the value of these units depends heavily on the underlying GPU architecture.

For instance, an NVIDIA GPU from the Ampere series may have fewer CUDA cores than a previous-generation Turing card but still offer better performance per watt and faster execution due to architectural enhancements. The same applies to AMD's stream processors in their RDNA architecture. The structure, instruction sets, and how these cores interact with memory and software drivers all contribute to the GPU's real-world efficiency. Intel's Xe cores are the newest to enter the field, and while still maturing, they show promise through integrated AI acceleration and flexible compute units.

Render output units (ROPs) and texture mapping units (TMUs) are two lesser-discussed but essential specifications. ROPs handle the final stage of pixel processing—taking all the calculations done by shaders and actually drawing them on the screen. More ROPs generally mean faster image output, especially in high-resolution rendering. TMUs, on the other hand, manage texture-related tasks such as mapping 2D images onto 3D models, applying filters, or performing mipmapping. A healthy number of TMUs ensures your games or graphics applications won't suffer lag or blurriness when dealing with complex scenes or detailed textures.

The increasing importance of AI and ray tracing acceleration in modern graphics applications also makes hardware like NVIDIA's Tensor and RT cores or AMD's Ray Accelerators worth examining. Tensor cores significantly enhance AI-driven features like DLSS (Deep Learning Super Sampling), which allows games to render at a lower resolution and upscale with machine learning for better frame rates without compromising image quality. Similarly, RT cores and AMD's equivalent units are designed to handle the intense computational load of ray tracing—simulating the behavior of light in real time. If you're into visually rich gaming or use software like Blender, Autodesk Arnold, or Unreal Engine, this hardware could be a necessity rather than a luxury.

Ray tracing and AI features don't just enhance visuals—they often dictate the longevity of your card. More games and professional applications are integrating these features, and choosing a GPU that lacks the necessary hardware could lead to obsolescence sooner than expected. That's why even if you're not using these technologies now, it may be worth considering cards that support them to extend your system's future viability.

Thermal management also connects directly with GPU performance. Some cards throttle—reduce their clock speed—when temperatures get too high, drastically reducing performance in the middle of demanding sessions. This is why TDP matters not just as a power metric but as an indicator of heat output. A GPU with a TDP of 300 watts needs robust thermal solutions and good airflow inside your PC case. Subpar thermal handling can degrade performance over time and potentially shorten the card's lifespan.

VR readiness and support for multi-monitor setups might not be listed as core specifications but can be critical for gamers and professionals alike. A GPU's ability to handle multiple 4K displays or power a VR headset without latency hinges on its memory bandwidth, port types, and GPU engine capabilities. Users aiming to create a productive workstation with three or more displays, or those interested in VR development, need to ensure the card's specs support these demands without strain.

Another often underestimated element is driver support and ecosystem maturity. NVIDIA, for example, is well-regarded for its comprehensive driver suite, including Studio Drivers for content creators and Game Ready Drivers for gamers. AMD has improved greatly with their Adrenalin software suite, but occasionally users still face longer wait times for optimized drivers post-launch. Intel, still the newcomer, is rapidly iterating but currently trails in ecosystem maturity. Solid drivers can mean the difference between smooth performance and frustrating compatibility issues.

Software optimization is another aspect that can dramatically affect performance but is often invisible to the average buyer. Certain games and applications are tuned to perform better with specific GPU architectures. For example, Adobe Premiere Pro and DaVinci Resolve may run better on NVIDIA cards due to CUDA acceleration. Similarly, some games are more compatible with AMD's FidelityFX suite. When selecting a GPU, it's worth researching how well your frequently used applications are optimized for the card you're considering.lighting calculations, and a variety of parallel processing tasks that define how quickly and efficiently your card can manage graphical data. When evaluating shader units or core counts, many users fall into the trap of thinking that a higher number automatically guarantees superior performance. But just like clock speed, the value of these units depends heavily on the underlying GPU architecture.

For instance, an NVIDIA GPU from the Ampere series may have fewer CUDA cores than a previous-generation Turing card but still offer better performance per watt and faster execution due to architectural enhancements. The same applies to AMD's stream processors in their RDNA architecture. The structure, instruction sets, and how these cores interact with memory and software drivers all contribute to the GPU's real-world efficiency. Intel's Xe cores are the newest to enter the field, and while still maturing, they show promise through integrated AI acceleration and flexible compute units.

Render output units (ROPs) and texture mapping units (TMUs) are two lesser-discussed but essential specifications. ROPs handle the final stage of pixel processing—taking all the calculations done by shaders and actually drawing them on the screen. More ROPs generally mean faster image output, especially in high-resolution rendering. TMUs, on the other hand, manage texture-related tasks such as mapping 2D images onto 3D models, applying filters, or performing mipmapping. A healthy number of TMUs ensures your games or graphics applications won't suffer lag or blurriness when dealing with complex scenes or detailed textures.

The increasing importance of AI and ray tracing acceleration in modern graphics applications also makes hardware like NVIDIA's Tensor and RT cores or AMD's Ray Accelerators worth examining. Tensor cores significantly enhance AI-driven features like DLSS (Deep Learning Super Sampling), which allows games to render at a lower resolution and upscale with machine learning for better frame rates without compromising image quality. Similarly, RT cores and AMD's equivalent units are designed to handle the intense computational load of ray tracing—simulating the behavior of light in real time. If you're into visually rich gaming or use software like Blender, Autodesk Arnold, or Unreal Engine, this hardware could be a necessity rather than a luxury.

Ray tracing and AI features don't just enhance visuals—they often dictate the longevity of your card. More games and professional applications are integrating these features, and choosing a GPU that lacks the necessary hardware could lead to obsolescence sooner than expected. That's why even if you're not using these technologies now, it may be worth considering cards that support them to extend your system's future viability.

Thermal management also connects directly with GPU performance. Some cards throttle—reduce their clock speed—when temperatures get too high, drastically reducing performance in the middle of demanding sessions. This is why TDP matters not just as a power metric but as an indicator of heat output. A GPU with a TDP of 300 watts needs robust thermal solutions and good airflow inside your PC case. Subpar thermal handling can degrade performance over time and potentially shorten the card's lifespan.

VR readiness and support for multi-monitor setups might not be listed as core specifications but can be critical for gamers and professionals alike. A GPU's ability to handle multiple 4K displays or power a VR headset without latency hinges on its memory bandwidth, port types, and GPU engine capabilities. Users aiming to create a productive workstation with three or more displays, or those interested in VR development, need to ensure the card's specs support these demands without strain.

Another often underestimated element is driver support and ecosystem maturity. NVIDIA, for example, is well-regarded for its comprehensive driver suite, including Studio Drivers for content creators and Game Ready Drivers for gamers. AMD has improved greatly with their Adrenalin software suite, but occasionally users still face longer wait times for optimized drivers post-launch. Intel, still the newcomer, is rapidly iterating but currently trails in ecosystem maturity. Solid drivers can mean the difference between smooth performance and frustrating compatibility issues.

Conclusion

In an age defined by visual fidelity, speed, and computational power, the graphics card has become more than just a component—it's the engine that powers our digital lives. From the thrilling realism of next-gen gaming to the precision of professional rendering, the subtlety of machine learning models, and the promise of virtual worlds yet to be built, GPUs shape what's possible on-screen and behind the scenes.

The journey through specifications, architectures, cooling solutions, emerging technologies, and real-world applications is no longer reserved for engineers and tech experts. The tools and knowledge now rest in the hands of consumers, creators, and professionals who recognize that a graphics card is not just a purchase—it's a strategic investment in performance, creativity, and capability.

Understanding how each feature fits into your workflow or gaming experience ensures that your hard-earned money is directed toward real value. Whether you're a passionate gamer seeking ultra-smooth frame rates, a content creator striving for render efficiency, or a researcher pushing the limits of AI computation, the right GPU choice can make the difference between average results and exceptional output.

The technology continues to evolve. Innovations like AI upscaling, cloud gaming, ray tracing, and energy-efficient designs are shaping a future where the line between software and hardware grows ever more intertwined. Staying informed is not just an option—it's the edge that keeps you adaptable and future-ready.

As new models release and benchmarks shift, one constant remains: the need to match your ambitions with the right technology. With the insights gained from this book, you're equipped to make those decisions—not just by specs on a page, but by understanding how those numbers translate into real-world impact.

So, whether you're building your dream PC, upgrading for the next wave of titles, or assembling a workstation for creative or scientific breakthroughs, you now carry the confidence to choose with purpose, to tune with precision, and to invest with clarity.

The power is in your hands—and the future is rendered by your choices.